VPJournals

TRAVEL JOURNAL

VPJournals

Travel Journal

St Lucia

VPJournals

ISBN-13: 978-1518846236
ISBN-10: 1518846238

Contact Details

Name:

Email address:

Tel:

Address:

Important Medical Information

Blood type:

Medication:

CONTENTS

Hi, I hope you enjoy this journal. It is packed with cool stuff and recommendations for you trip to St Lucia, and has plenty of space to record details of your trip.

Have fun in St Lucia

Great Places to visit in St Lucia

Morne Coubaril Estate	✓
Pigeon Island National Park	
Anse Mamin	
Latille Waterfalls and Gardens	
Diamond Botanical Gardens	
Marigot Bay	
Jalousie Beach	
Sulphur Springs	
Soufriere Marine Management Area	
La Soufriere Drive-In Volcano	
Mamiku Gardens	
Rodney Bay Marina	

Church of the Assumption	
Maria Islands Nature Reserve	
Diamond Mineral Baths	
Anse Couchon	
Mount Gimie	
Cape Moule a Chique	
Union Nature Center	
Morne Fortune	
Melting Pot West Indian Studio	
Canaries	
Island Riders	
Brig Unicorn	
Our Planet Centre	

Cool Places to visit in St Lucia with Kids

Pigeon Island Museum and Interpretive Center	✓
Marigot Bay	
Island Riders	
Brig Unicorn	
Our Planet Centre	
Debarras Turtle Watch	
Mount Soufriere	
Treetop Adventure Park	
Rainforest Hike	
Mamiku Gardens	
Diamond Falls Botanical Gardens	
Sulphur Springs Park	

Latille Waterfalls and Gardens	
Church of the Assumption	
Union Nature Center	
Melting Pot West Indian Studio	
Dennery	
Marquis Estate	
Eudovic's Art Studio	
Inniskilling Fusiliers Monument	
Derek Walcott Square	
Zaka Art Cafe	
La Soufriere Drive-In Volcano	
Jalousie Beach	

Good Places to Eat in St Lucia

Spice of India	✓
The Pink Plantation House	
Orlando's Restaurant & Bar	
Rainforest Hideaway	
Flavours of the Grill	
Martha's Tables	
The Coal Pot	
Big Chef Steak House	
The Mango Tree	
Delirius	
The Naked Fisherman Bar and Grill	
The Reef Beach Cafe	

Julietta's	
Tapas on the Bay	
The Old Plantation Yard	
Jada's Tropical Water Ice	
Roots Bar	
Fox Grove Inn	
Rowley's	
Club Whispers Restaurant & Bar	
Masala Bay	
Brown Sugar Restaurant & Bar	
The Beacon Restaurant	
Felly Belly	
Windsong Restaurant	

Best Websites to Research Further

Do some more research on the internet to plan your trip:

stlucianow.com
www.geographia.com/st-lucia
www.saintluciauk.org
www.lonelyplanet.com/st-lucia
www.wikitravel.org/en/Saint_Lucia
www.nytimes.com/travel/guides/caribbean-and-bermuda/st-lucia/overview.html
www.caribya.com/st.lucia/
www.nomadicmatt.com/travel-guides/caribbean-travel-tips/st-lucia/
www.wikipedia.org/wiki/Saint_Lucia

More places I want to visit on our trip

1. ______
2. ______
3. ______
4. ______
5. ______
6. ______
7. ______
8. ______
9. ______
10. ______
11. ______
12. ______
13. ______
14. ______
15. ______

Postcard List

Name:
Address:

Name:
Address:

Name:
Address:

Name:

Address:

Name:

Address:

Name:

Address:

Name:

Address:

Name:
Address:

Name:
Address:

Name:
Address:

Name:
Address:

Name:

Address:

Name:

Address:

Name:

Address:

Packing List

✓	This Journal
	Tickets
	Passport
	Money
	Chargers
	Batteries
	Book to read
	Camera
	Tablet
	Sun glasses
	Sun cream

	Toiletries
	Water
	Watch
	Snacks
	Umbrella
	Towel
	Guide book
	Kindle
	Jacket
	Medication
	Add more below

St Lucia Facts

- Saint Lucia is an island nation in the Caribbean Sea. The island is considered part of the Windward Islands and gets its name from the French who named it after St. Lucy of Syracuse

- In 1979 Saint Lucia became a fully independent country although the country still considers Queen Elizabeth II its queen

- It covers a land area of 617 km^2 (238.23 sq miles) and has a population of 174,000 people. Castries is the capital city

- The control of St Lucia switched from the French to English many times in the 17th and 18th centuries. In 1814, Britain took control of the island

- St Lucia became an independent state on 22nd February 1979. This day is a public holiday in St Lucia

- One of St Lucia's main export is bananas, but they also export beer and petroleum oils

- Tourism is very important to the St Lucian economy. Many people come to St Lucia every year to see the peaks of The Pitons or to visit the drive-in volcano at Sulphur Springs (Soufriere). Many tourists come to St Lucia as part of a Caribbean cruise

- About 300,000 people visit Saint Lucia every year

- It used to be known as the Island of the Iguanas by the earliest settlers, the Amerindian Arawak and Carib people

- St. Lucia is home to one of the most remarkable distilleries, Roseau Valley, which is famous for producing more than 21 types of rum to sample or purchase. Located on Rodney Bay, it has stood in this location for decades

- Despite a population of only 176,000, Saint Lucians have won two Nobel Prizes: Arthur Lewis (economics) and Derek Walcott (literature)

- "The Land, The People, The Light" was coined as the national motto of St. Lucia when it obtained total independence from England on 22nd February, 1979

- During the mid-1960s, St. Lucia's biggest cultivation was of sugarcane, which was replaced by the cultivation of banana

Clothes & Shoe Sizes

Children's Shoe Sizes

UK	EUROPE	US	Japan
4	20	4½ or 5	12 ½
4 ½	21	5 or 5½	13
5	21 or 22	5½ or 6	13 ½
5 ½	22	6	13½ or 14
6	23	6½ or 7	14 or 14½
6 ½	23 or 24	7 ½	14½ or 15
7	24	7½ or 8	15
7 ½	25	8 or 9	15 ½
8	25 or 26	8½ or 9	16
8 ½	26	9½	16 ½
9	27	9½ or 10	16 ½ or 17
10	28	10½ or 11	17 ½
10½ or 11	29	11½ or 12	18
11 ½	30	12½	18 or 18 ½
12	31	13	19 or 19 ½
12 ½	31	13 or 13½	19 ½ or 20
13	32	1	20
13 ½	32 ½	1 ½	20 ½
1	33	1½ or 2	21
2	34	2½ or 3	22

Children's Clothing Sizes

UK	EUROPE	US	Australia
12m	80cm	12-18m	12m
18m	80-86cm	18-24m	18m
24m	86-92cm	23-24m	2
2-3	92-98cm	2T	3
3-4	98-104cm	4T	4
3-5	104-110cm	5	5
5-6	110-116cm	6	6
6-7	116-122cm	6X-7	7
7-8	122-128cm	7 to 8	8
8-9	128-134cm	9 to 10	9
9-10	134-140cm	10	10
10-11	140-146cm	11	11
11-12	146-152cm	14	12

Women's Shoe Sizes

UK	EUROPE	US	Japan
3	35 ½	5	22 ½
3 ½	36	5 ½	23
4	37	6	23
4 ½	37 ½	6 ½	23 ½
5	38	7	24
5 ½	39	7 ½	24
6	39 ½	8	24 ½
6 ½	40	8 ½	25
7	41	9 ½	25 ½
7 ½	41 ½	10	26
8	42	10 ½	26 ½

Women's Clothes Sizes

UK	US	Japan	France / Spain	Germany	St Lucia	Australia
6/8	6	7-9	36	34	40	8
10	8	9-11	38	36	42	10
12	10	11-13	40	38	44	12
14	12	13-15	42	39	46	14
16	14	15-17	44	40	48	16
18	16	17-19	46	42	50	18
20	18	19-21	48	44	52	20

Men's Shoe Sizes

UK	EUROPE	US	Japan
6	38 ½	6 ½	24 ½
6 ½	39	7	25
7	40	7 ½	25 ½
7 ½	41	8	26
8	42	8 ½	27 ½
8 ½	43	9	27 ½
9	43 ½	9 ½	28
9 ½	44	10	28 ½
10	44	10 ½	28 ½
10 ½	44 ½	11	29
11	45	12	29 ½

Men's Suit / Coat / Sweater Sizes

UK / US / Aus	EU / Japan	General
32	42	Small
34	44	Small
36	46	Small
38	48	Medium
40	50	Large
42	52	Large
44	54	Extra Large
46	56	Extra Large

Men's Pants / Trouser Sizes (Waist)

UK / US	Europe
32	81 cm
34	86 cm
36	91 cm
38	97 cm
40	102 cm
42	107 cm

We have included another copy of this at the back of the book, so you can find it quickly again when you are in St Lucia

St Lucia Trip Diary

Write a daily diary during your trip

Day 1

Date: ____________ **Weather:** ____________

Day 2

Date: ______________ **Weather:** ______________

Day 3

Date: ____________ **Weather:** ____________

Day 4

Date: ______________ **Weather:** ______________

Day 5

Tip! Send your postcards

Date: ____________ **Weather:** ____________

Day 6

Date: ____________ **Weather:** ____________

Day 7

Date: __________ **Weather:** __________

Day 8

Date: ________________ **Weather:** ________________

Day 9

Date: **Weather:**

Day 10

Date: **Weather:**

Day 11

Date: ________________ **Weather:** ________________

Day 12

Date: ____________ **Weather:** ____________

Day 13

Date: ______________ **Weather:** ______________

Day 14

Date: ____________ **Weather:** ____________

Day 15

Date: ____________ **Weather:** ____________

Day 16

Date: ______________ **Weather:** ______________

Day 17

Date: ____________ **Weather:** ____________

Day 18

Date: ________________ **Weather:** ________________

Day 19

Date: ____________ **Weather:** ____________

Day 20

Date: ____________________ **Weather:** ____________________

Day 21

Date: **Weather:**

Memories of your Trip

Things I will remember from the trip

Favorite Places visited on the Trip

People I Met

Name:
Address:
Tel:
email:

Name:
Address:
Tel:
email:

Name:
Address:
Tel:
email:

Name:
Address:
Tel:
email:

Name:
Address:
Tel:
email:

Name:
Address:
Tel:
email:

Name:
Address:
Tel:
email:

Name:
Address:
Tel:
email:

Name:
Address:
Tel:
email:

Name:
Address:
Tel:
email:

Name:
Address:
Tel:
email:

We hope you enjoyed your trip to St Lucia

Please leave us a review if you found this Journal useful

Check out our useful resources on the next few pages

Clothes & Shoe Sizes

Children's Shoe Sizes

UK	EUROPE	US	Japan
4	20	4½ or 5	12 ½
4 ½	21	5 or 5½	13
5	21 or 22	5½ or 6	13 ½
5 ½	22	6	13½ or 14
6	23	6½ or 7	14 or 14½
6 ½	23 or 24	7 ½	14½ or 15
7	24	7½ or 8	15
7 ½	25	8 or 9	15 ½
8	25 or 26	8½ or 9	16
8 ½	26	9½	16 ½
9	27	9½ or 10	16 ½ or 17
10	28	10½ or 11	17 ½
10½ or 11	29	11½ or 12	18
11 ½	30	12½	18 or 18 ½
12	31	13	19 or 19 ½
12 ½	31	13 or 13½	19 ½ or 20
13	32	1	20
13 ½	32 ½	1 ½	20 ½
1	33	1½ or 2	21
2	34	2½ or 3	22

Children's Clothing Sizes

UK	EUROPE	US	Australia
12m	80cm	12-18m	12m
18m	80-86cm	18-24m	18m
24m	86-92cm	23-24m	2
2-3	92-98cm	2T	3
3-4	98-104cm	4T	4
3-5	104-110cm	5	5
5-6	110-116cm	6	6
6-7	116-122cm	6X-7	7
7-8	122-128cm	7 to 8	8
8-9	128-134cm	9 to 10	9
9-10	134-140cm	10	10
10-11	140-146cm	11	11
11-12	146-152cm	14	12

Women's Shoe Sizes

UK	EUROPE	US	Japan
3	35 ½	5	22 ½
3 ½	36	5 ½	23
4	37	6	23
4 ½	37 ½	6 ½	23 ½
5	38	7	24
5 ½	39	7 ½	24
6	39 ½	8	24 ½
6 ½	40	8 ½	25
7	41	9 ½	25 ½
7 ½	41 ½	10	26
8	42	10 ½	26 ½

Women's Clothes Sizes

UK	US	Japan	France / Spain	Germany	St Lucia	Australia
6/8	6	7-9	36	34	40	8
10	8	9-11	38	36	42	10
12	10	11-13	40	38	44	12
14	12	13-15	42	39	46	14
16	14	15-17	44	40	48	16
18	16	17-19	46	42	50	18
20	18	19-21	48	44	52	20

Men's Shoe Sizes

UK	EUROPE	US	Japan
6	38 ½	6 ½	24 ½
6 ½	39	7	25
7	40	7 ½	25 ½
7 ½	41	8	26
8	42	8 ½	27 ½
8 ½	43	9	27 ½
9	43 ½	9 ½	28
9 ½	44	10	28 ½
10	44	10 ½	28 ½
10 ½	44 ½	11	29
11	45	12	29 ½

Men's Suit / Coat / Sweater Sizes

UK / US / Aus	EU / Japan	General
32	42	Small
34	44	Small
36	46	Small
38	48	Medium
40	50	Large
42	52	Large
44	54	Extra Large
46	56	Extra Large

Men's Pants / Trouser Sizes (Waist)

UK / US	Europe
32	81 cm
34	86 cm
36	91 cm
38	97 cm
40	102 cm
42	107 cm

Common Translations

English	French	Spanish	Italian
Hello	Bonjour	Hola	Ciao
Goodbye	Au revoir	Adiós	Arrivederci
Yes	Oui	Sí	Si
No	Non	No	No
Please	S'il-vous-plaît	Por favor	Per favore
Thank you	Merci	Gracias	Grazie
Excuse me	Excusez-moi	Perdón	Mi scusi
How much	Combien	Cuánto	Quanto
My name is	Mon nom est	Mi nombre es	Io mi chiamo
Where is	Où est	Dónde está	Dov'è
The bank	La banque	El banco	La banca
The toilet	Les toilettes	El baño	Il bagno

German	**Japanese**	**Mandarin**	**Hindi**
Hallo	Kon'nichiwa	Ni hao	Namaste
Auf Wiedersehen	Sayonara	Zaijian	Alavida
Ja	Hai	Shi de	Ham
Nein	Ie	Meiyou	Nahim
Bitte	Onegaishimasu	Qing	Krpaya
Vielen Dank	Arigato	Xiexie	Dhan'yavada
Entschuldigung	Sumimasen	Duoshao	Mujhe mapha karem
Wie viel	Ikura	Wo de mingzi shi	Kitana
Mein Name ist	Watashinonamaeha	Nali	Mera nama hai
Wo ist	Doko ni aru	Yinhang	Kaham hai
Die Bank	Ginko	Yinhang	Bainka
Die Toilette	Toire	Cesuo	Saucalaya

Notes:

Made in the USA
Coppell, TX
10 December 2019

12723207R00077